YOUR BRAIN HEALTH LIFESTYLE

LIFESTYLE

A Proactive Program to Preserve Your Life Story

YOUR BRAIN HEALTH LIFESTYLE

LIFESTYLE

A Proactive Program to Preserve Your Life Story

Paul David Nussbaum, Ph.D.
Clinical Neuropsychologist and Adjunct
Associate Professor
Neurological Surgery
University of Pittsburgh School of Medicine
(412) 471-1195
ageon@zoominternet.net
paulnussbaum.com

ISBN 10: 1-59571-184-8
ISBN 13: 978-1-59571-184-7
Library of Congress Control Number: 2007923129

Word Association Publishers
205 5th Avenue
Tarentum, PA 15084
www.wordassociation.com

TABLE OF CONTENTS

Dedicated to the Human Brain!

YOUR BRAIN HEALTH LIFESTYLE

"You have no greater asset than your life story. It must be shared with your next great generation, the little ones in your life"

INTRODUCTION: THE EMERGENCE OF BRAIN HEALTH

During the past decade I have traveled the nation speaking about the mystery and miracle of the human brain. My talks are delivered to groups and organizations both small and large. From basements of small churches to the National Press Club and beyond the enthusiasm for learning about the human brain has been remarkable. It is personally pleasing to see the increase in popularity of the human brain and the emergence of a serious directive to develop health policy and programs for this essential part of our being. We are truly engaged in a cultural shift towards brain health that has already witnessed new products, new programs, and new companies geared to the human brain.

Our society is indeed undergoing a not-so-quiet revolution regarding the human brain and brain health. The concept of brain health is now discussed in major sectors of society including personal development, health care, business, media and even religion. It is quite common to see information on brain health in major news outlets, popular magazines, peer-reviewed medical journals, business periodicals, initial public offerings, and even a new television series. This is good news because it indicates a cultural shift in which the United States is prepared and willing to begin the process of integrating brain health into our language and more importantly into our daily health regimen.

I have had the unique opportunity to travel the nation the past decade discussing the basics of the human brain and teaching audiences from all backgrounds what the research suggests we can do to improve our brain health. There is without exception a genuine enthusiasm from Americans to learn about their own brain and how to keep their brain healthy. Some of this enthusiasm may be steeped in fear, a real concern of losing mental intellect and memory as we get older. The enthusiasm, however, is also based on a healthy desire to remain healthy. Perhaps most gratifying to me is the fact that the message of brain health, when explained correctly, resonates with persons from all backgrounds. The reason is rather simple: people want information that will benefit their health and our society is more invested in lifestyle and health than ever before.

One of the great paradoxes of our time is the fact that the human brain is the single greatest, most magnificent system ever designed in the history of the universe! Simultaneously, most Americans do not know the basics of their own brain and therefore they cannot take care of their brain. A recent survey of Americans on brain health sponsored by MetLife Foundation and the American Society on Aging (*www.asaging.org*) found only 3% identified brain health as a leading health topic. More promising, the same survey found a majority (88%) believe they can keep their brains fit and nearly 90% believe regular checkups for their brain are important. Americans also demonstrate a decent understanding of what activities are considered good for brain health. In order for our nation to be enlightened about brain health we need to do a better job educating our citizens about the human brain and I believe this education should begin early in life.

The United States has done a good job educating the public about the importance of cardiac or heart health. We decided to prioritize heart health because many of our loved ones have cardiac illness and it represents a primary cause of death. Some research indicates that while cardiac illness remains a leading cause of death inroads have been made to slow the rate of cardiac-caused premature death. We have persistent educational campaigns to teach the public about behaviors that promote cardiac health. Consider the recent introduction of aerobic centers, exercise clubs and television programs on exercise. Grocery stores and our nation's restaurants have sections dedicated to heart healthy foods. There are even icons of red hearts that identify for the consumer those foods that promote heart health.

Our culture has also adopted a general fondness of the heart as a favorite organ in our body. Like the ancient Egyptians we have a belief that our being revolves around the heart. Our language contains many statements that give the heart meaning it really does not deserve. For example, statements such as "I love you with all my heart", "the Steelers played their hearts out", and "you broke my heart" suggest our heart has the capacity for emotion or feelings. Indeed, the human heart is a pump that perfuses blood throughout the body. It has no emotion like love, thought, or motor skill related to it. All of the emotions and thoughts that we relate to the heart are really owned by the brain. In this regard, our brains have not been treated fairly and I believe it is time we begin to show our brain a little love and attention it deserves. We are so lucky to be alive at this period in our nation's history. We have an unprecedented opportunity to be part of a societal shift toward brain health that will likely lead to an unleashing of human potential and maybe a reduction in brain disease. Some of our advances may occur in the development of traditional medical interventions such as development of a vaccine or new medication therapy. Gene therapy and stem cell research with use of our own stem cells to combat disease may offer an entire new frontier of treatment or prevention options. The other major advancement is a new national priority to the human brain that declares our desire to address the fact that we are losing many of our family members to brain disease. Similar to our approach to cardiac health, the United States can become an enlightened society on brain health by implementing a national lifelong educational program on the basics of the human brain. Preventative programs can adopt and pay for a brain health lifestyle for all of us and the development of brain health centers that recognize and offer research-based activities for the consumer can emerge. Our grocery stores and restaurants can begin the process of identifying for the consumer foods that have brain health promoting effects. Businesses that cater to the vitality of the human brain and our cognitive/emotional abilities will continue to emerge.

A nation that prioritizes brain health understands that a lifelong and proactive lifestyle is needed. Individuals must educate themselves about their own brain and begin to make the behavioral changes necessary to develop as healthy a brain as possible. Corporate America, businesses, media and television, and health care systems can promote brain health in their own specialized ways and our daily language will reflect a society that embraces the importance of caring for our brain. This is my third book to champion brain health as a national priority and to continue my effort to educate America about the importance of basic brain education. I believe you will care for your brain if you learn the basics of your brain. This book will educate you about this miraculous part of your being. You will have fun reading this book because I know you will take interest in yourself. The book then provides you with a proactive lifestyle for brain health. The lifestyle provides five important components and the research-based activities that can be organized within each component. As you read the book think about yourself and your current thoughts about your brain. Review your current lifestyle and make critical decisions regarding necessary changes to promote the health of your brain.

Once you have read this book you will know more about the human brain than most Americans. More importantly, you will know what behaviors are important to promote your own brain health. This knowledge will help you take the steps to change your current behavior and adopt the proactive lifestyle for brain health. This is not easy and it is not a "quick fix." This is a long process that will be difficult and filled with self inspection and challenge. I have found personal satisfaction in my own behavioral change as I work to integrate brain health into my life. I also have fun with others as we work together to adopt brain health changes. This should be fun and remember you are working on yourself. It is time for you to consider your brain and how to keep it healthy!

COOL STUFF ABOUT YOUR BRAIN

Your brain weighs 2 to 4 pounds and is made up of Gray Matter and White Matter. The Gray Matter tends to be contained in an area of your brain called the *cortex*, a word that translates to mean "bark of a tree." Your cortex (see illustration #1) is a convoluted mass of cells with folds and flaps that sits snug within your skull.

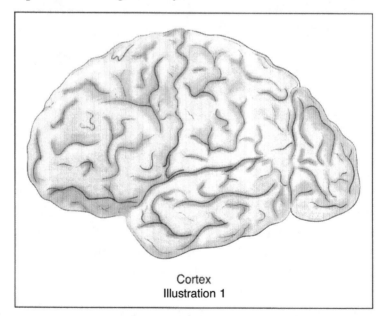

Cortex
Illustration 1

It developed from the back to the front meaning the front part of your cortex is the youngest member or region of your brain. The cortex is primarily responsible for your most complex thinking abilities including memory, language, planning, concept formation, problem solving, spatial representation, auditory and visual processing, mood and personality. Processing in the cortex tends to be conscious and intentional.

The cortex is generally organized by four primary regions or lobes: Frontal Lobe, Temporal Lobe, Parietal Lobe, and Occipital Lobe (see illustration # 2). Each of these four lobes has specific behaviors and functions primary to its region. For example the frontal lobe is also known as the *executive system* since it helps execute behavior, organizes behavior, plans, conceptualizes, maintains cognitive flexibility, and mood stability. Your personality is thought to reside in the frontal region of your brain. Your temporal lobe is the site of your auditory brain, memory and new learning, language, and perhaps religiosity. Your parietal lobes help you with orientation to space, memory, reading and writing, mathematics, and appreciation of left versus right. Finally, your occipital lobes help you to see, discriminate what you see, and to perceive.

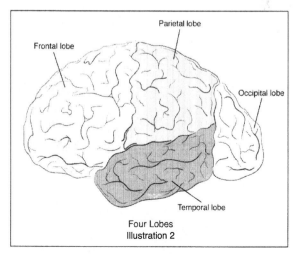

Four Lobes
Illustration 2

Sitting just under the cortex and on top of the ascending brain stem are a number of smaller and generally more primitive structures (relative to the cortex) known as the *subcortex*. Your subcortex primarily processes rote skills and procedures. Some, if not most of the processing conducted in the subcortex is subconscious. Functions such as driving, dressing, typing, etc. involve multiple rote procedures that are conducted at a subconscious level. Your subcortex and cortex are distinct regions of the brain, but they do not sit in isolation of one another. In fact, there are numerous connections between these two important brain regions. The brain operates as a symphony with numerous and distinct regions harmonizing perfectly as one unit.

Another way to learn about your brain is to consider the fact that your brain has two sides. We refer to these sides as hemispheres and you have a left hemisphere and a right hemisphere (see illustration #3).

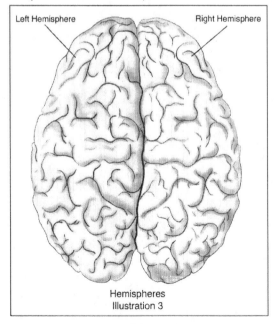

Hemispheres
Illustration 3

Interestingly, your behaviors and functions are related primarily to one of these two hemispheres. For example, most of us and nearly all right handers have language distributed primarily in the left hemisphere. We refer to the hemisphere with language as the *dominant hemisphere* as a sign of our respect to the importance of language. Left handed persons with a parent who is left handed (relatively rare) have a higher probability than the right handers of having language distributed primarily in the right hemisphere. They would be *right hemisphere dominant*.

Your dominant hemisphere (left for most of us) also processes details, is task oriented, logical, analytical, and sequences information. Most of western civilization is built around the left hemisphere as our classrooms are set up in rows and columns of chairs and our cities tend to have tall building in rows and columns. We tend to focus more on the detail and less on the gestalt. Your *non-dominant hemisphere* helps you process non language information such as size, shapes, sounds, and space. Your ability to navigate in space to locate your car in a parking garage or get home from a walk is an example of non-dominant function. Likewise, your ability to appreciate distinct sounds such as a baby's cry or a fire alarm tends to be a process of the non-dominant hemisphere.

Your two hemispheres are connected by a bridge of cells referred to as the *corpus collosum*. Information crosses from one side of your brain to the other over the corpus collosum and this is a critical part of your brain's ability to remain so functional despite its many complex operations on a daily basis. Interestingly, the female brain is thought to have a larger corpus collosum and underscores the notion that female brains process information differently than men.

Females tend to utilize both sides of their brains more to process than men who rely primarily on one side, the dominant hemisphere. It is probably not coincidental that audiences across the nation always respond with same answer to my question "what is a common behavior that men and women struggle with on a daily basis?" The answer is communication!

The operation and function of your brain is ultimately conducted by the millions of brain cells we refer to as *neurons.* A neuron (see illustration #4) contains a cell body sometimes referred to as a *soma,* a long arm extending out from the cell body referred to as an *axon*, and branch like figures called *dendrites* that extend out into the brain environment seeking new information to relay back to the cell body.

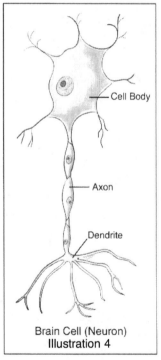

Brain Cell (Neuron)
Illustration 4

Indeed information from the cell body travels down the axon into the surrounding brain while information from the environment is gathered by the dendrites and brought back to the cell body. This ongoing exchange of information by the brain is why we refer to it as the *central information processing system.*

We are taught that our brains contain millions of brain cells and that each neuron can communicate with another 10,000 neurons. Interestingly, one neuron never touches another neuron, but two cells may communicate via chemicals and this chemical marriage is called a *synapse.* The more synaptic connections you develop over your lifespan the healthier your brain may be because it is building up **brain reserve**. Brain reserve, as you will learn about below, may have the ability to delay the onset of neurodegenerative diseases such as Alzheimer's Disease (AD.)

The miracle is that your brain is dynamic and continues to be shaped and to develop. It has *plasticity.* As such, there is no finite capacity or limitation. In this way your brain is very distinct and actually much superior to the fanciest of all computers because computers will always have built in limitations and finite capacity. Your dynamic brain is shaped by environmental input across your lifespan beginning in the womb. There really is no critical period of brain development unless one considers life itself to be the measure. As you will learn in the next section of this book, the type of environmental input to your brain can make a difference regarding the health of your brain. You do have some control and this is great news!

When I give lectures to the public I always want my audience to personalize the message. This story is, after all, about you and your brain. It really does not get any more personal. Learning about oneself can be fun and challenging. There is one part of your brain that I emphasize because this structure, *the hippocampus,* is so critical to you and **your life story**. The hippocampus (see illustration #5) sits in the middle of each temporal lobe that lies under your temples on each side of your head.

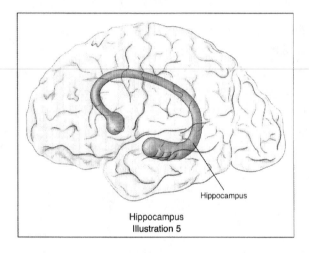

Hippocampus

Hippocampus
Illustration 5

Your hippocampus or hippocampi for plural, as you have one in each hemisphere, takes new information in and maintains the information in a type of working buffer. If you believe the information is important and you need to store the information for an extended period of time, your hippocampus will transition the information to a specific area of your cortex. This process is not random, but rather very sophisticated as the process of storage seems to be stimulus-based. That is, if you are learning information that is visual your hippocampus will help store that information permanently in the visual cortex of the brain. The same process is thought to occur for the other four types of sensory input.

Your hippocampi represent your vital learning and encoding structures thereby helping you to build **your life story** and maintain your personal memories. Alzheimer's disease (AD) is a leading cause of dementia and the disease destroys very early the hippocampi of the brain. As a result, those inflicted with this terrible brain disease cannot learn new information and they typically will repeat. As you will learn in the next section of this book, your hippocampi are critical structures to the story of brain health. Recent research suggests your hippocampi have tremendous ability including new brain cell development referred to as *neurogenesis*.

You now know more than most Americans about the human brain. You have now personalized this critical part of your being and you should feel empowered and excited to learn more. If you cannot get excited about yourself there is a problem! Let us review some important information about the basics of your brain:

1. Your brain weighs 2 to 4 pounds.
2. Your brain is comprised of at least 60% fat. It is the fattest system in your body.
3. Every heart beat provides 25% of the blood and oxygen to your brain.
4. Your brain has a Cortex and a Subcortex.
5. Your brain has a left (primarily language) and a right hemisphere (non-language functions).
6. Your hippocampus (i) encodes new information and initiates learning and memory.
7. You have millions of brain cells (called neurons) that can be shaped and increased in number with exposure to complex and novel environments.

8. Neurons communicate with each other chemically referred to as a synapse.
9. The more synaptic connections the greater your brain reserve.
10. Brain reserve is thought to delay the onset of diseases such as AD.

How Your Brain Health Works

Now that you have learned about your brain I hope you understand the unique asset and miracle that sits within your own skull. Your 2 to 4 pound brain is the true portable and wireless device in the universe! You have learned about the structure or hardware of your brain. Now it is important you learn about the power of your brain and how it can be shaped and nurtured across your entire lifespan. We refer to the dynamic, constantly reorganizing, and malleable nature of your brain as *brain plasticity*. Please understand that your brain is not a rigid or static system with a limited capacity or finite critical period for development. The power of brain plasticity permits you to implement a lifelong and proactive program to grow and promote your own brain health.

Environment and the Rat Brain

To better understand why brain plasticity is important to you we can discuss the basic findings of animal brain research. In the 1950s research was conducted to investigate whether environment had any effect on the structure and function of the animal brain. Researchers designed a study with rodents raised in two distinct environments: *enriched environment versus un-enriched environment*. Rodents were raised in one of these two environments and then their brains were analyzed and compared at autopsy. Results yielded significant differences in the brains of these rodents. Specifically, rodents raised in an enriched environment had a larger cortex, more cellular connections (called a synapse that leads to brain reserve), and new brain cells (called neurogenesis) in the hippocampus (structure critical to new learning and memory).

I became interested in this work and I wanted to know how researchers defined an enriched environment. My review of this work (see Brain Health and Wellness, 2003) suggested three factors were critical to the enriched environment. They included (1) *socialization*: animals had to have other animals of its kind in the environment; (2) *physical activity*: animals had a running wheel to exercise on; and (3) *mental stimulation*: there were toys in the environment animals could play and interact with. Animals raised in un-enriched environments were raised in isolation, had no running wheel, and had no toys to play with. While this research offered highly significant and important findings regarding the effect of the environment on brain structure in the animal, the critical issue of whether the same findings could be established for humans remained unknown.

Environment and the Human Brain

It was not until 1998 that a landmark study found the human brain to have the ability to develop new brain cells. This study was a threshold moment for our species as it confronted our long tradition of believing the human brain to be a rigid system with no ability to generate new brain cells. We had always believed the brain is born with all of its brain cells, that the human brain loses brain cells on a daily basis, and that our brains do not generate or replace the lost cells with new ones. The study also indicated that the new brain cells were generated in the human hippocampus, the same area neurogenesis was found in the animal brain. Today, research is ongoing to determine if neurogenesis occurs in other regions of the human brain or if it is something specific to the hippocampus. New brain cell development is one outcome of a brain with plasticity. Recall that plasticity refers to a brain that is dynamic, constantly reorganizing, and malleable. The human brain therefore is now thought to possess the same type of neural plasticity as the rodent brain. Interestingly, the animal studies were conducted on rodents across their lifespan with an equivalent human age of seventy or eighty. A human brain that generates new brain cells mandates a curiosity of how this wonderful adaptive ability occurs. We can return to the animal studies to derive some answers to this question. Recall that the enriched environment led to new brain cell development in the hippocampus of the animal. The three critical factors important to the enriched environment included socialization, physical activity, and mental stimulation. It makes good sense, therefore, to ask if the human brain can be similarly affected by environment and if the enriched environment promotes positive brain changes in the human.

As you will read in the next section there is good reason to believe that the human brain benefits from a novel and complex environment. It is also important to know that the first potential enriched environment is the womb and that the type of environment you expose your brain to will have consequences at every age across your lifespan. The miracle of brain plasticity does not end at a particular age. Indeed, the human brain probably does not know its chronological age and will demand and benefit from enriched environments at every age. The major point of this section is that you are strongly encouraged and empowered to expose your brain to the novel and complex every day regardless of your age!

The Importance of Brain Reserve

Brain reserve is a well known concept that refers to a build up of brain cell connections (synaptic density) that serves to assist the brain in the battle against neurodegenerative diseases. To better understand brain reserve, consider the following simplistic analogy that I use in my lectures on the human brain. Imagine flying in an airplane nearly 1000 feet above the ground. As you peer out your window down to the ground you will see two very distinct scenes. The first scene is a jungle where there are so many trees you cannot see the ground. The second scene is an island with one palm tree blowing slowly in the wind. You want your brain to be like the jungle where you have a tremendous number of synaptic connections. This is referred to as *synaptic density* and is a direct measure of brain reserve. You do not want your brain to look like the island with one palm tree. The reason is also simple. If you consider AD or other types of dementia or brain disease as a weed-whacker, the disease will invade the brain and begin to cut down the neurons and synaptic connections. This occurs just like a weed-whacker cutting through the weeds around your house. If your brain looks like a jungle, filled with synaptic connections, it will take AD and other diseases a long time to show its ugly clinical face. However, if your brain looks like the island with one palm tree the clinical signs of AD will manifest quickly because there is no reserve to fight it off.

Indeed, some research has shown that even though brains are diagnosed with AD at autopsy due to the presence of neuropathological changes, a significant number of these persons never demonstrated the clinical aspects of the disease in life. This is explained one way using the brain reserve concept. That is, persons who never manifested AD in life, even though they had the neuropathologic characteristics in their brain at autopsy, had built up brain reserve to fight off or delay the onset of the disease.

The power of brain reserve is further supported by findings that relate higher education and occupational levels to lower risk of AD. For those with high education or occupation levels who do manifest AD, their presentation of the disease occurs later than those without similar backgrounds, and once the disease manifests the person dies soon after. The reason for this is that the when the disease presents clinically it is already advanced into the final stage because the person's brain reserve had been fighting it off.

Education and occupation are two examples of environments that can be enriched or not. You expose your brain to the education and occupation environment frequently across your lifespan. Each of these two environments provides the opportunity for you to engage in a novel and complex setting that promotes the development of brain reserve. To the extent that these environments or other settings become rote and passive, brain reserve will not be as developed and the overall health benefit for your brain is not as great. It is your personal challenge to expose your brain to the novel and complex, the enriched environment on a daily basis. Studies suggest the earlier in life you begin your exposure to the enriched environment the greater the health benefit to your brain even into late life. This finding is supported by research that demonstrates a relationship between poverty in childhood and increased risk of AD later in life, higher IQ in childhood and young adulthood and reduced risk of AD later in life, language development in young adulthood and reduced risk of neuropathologic changes in the brain at autopsy, and a passive lifestyles in the 40s to increased risk of AD later in life.

These findings on humans support the idea that diseases of the brain that manifest late in life may actually begin early in life. Further, these findings suggest we can become involved very early in life with a proactive lifestyle that promotes brain health and that helps to reduce the risk of AD and related dementias later in life. It is important to prioritize a proactive lifestyle for brain health regardless of your age, to embrace the power of brain plasticity and development of brain reserve, and to have fun in the process of caring for your brain!

What have you learned in this section? Here is a quick review:

1. The animal brain has the ability to generate new brain cells, particularly in the hippocampus.
2. The animal brain demonstrates positive effects from being exposed to an enriched environment.
3. The enriched environment for the animal includes socialization, physical activity, and mental stimulation.
4. In 1998 we learned the human brain also has the ability to generate new brain cells. Identical to the

animal brain, humans generate new brain cells in the hippocampus.

5. Your brain, therefore, has plasticity, and the ability to be shaped by environment at any age.

6. By exposing your brain to the enriched environment, the novel and complex, you build up your brain reserve.

7. Brain reserve is thought to fight off or delay the onset of brain disease.

8. It is important for you to engage in a proactive and lifelong lifestyle that promotes brain health to maintain **your life story**!

YOUR BRAIN HEALTH LIFESTYLE PROGRAM

Your brain is a highly dynamic and constantly reorganizing system capable of being shaped across your entire lifespan. Similar to animals, your brain can generate new brain cells and respond to environmental input. **Your goal is to expose your brain to enriched environments, to the novel and complex, and to grow your brain reserve!** Stimuli that is considered rote and passive to your brain is most likely not as health promoting. We learned from animal brain research that an enriched environment has three critical factors: *socialization, physical activity, and mental stimulation*. It makes perfect sense to consider these same critical factors as important to the human brain. As part of my work on human brain health I have proposed a lifestyle that includes **five critical factors** (three from the animal research and two additional factors):

1. Socialization
2. Physical Activity
3. Mental Stimulation
4. Spirituality
5. Nutrition

Each of these factors is necessary to your *brain health program* and together they form an *integrated whole* for you. The five factors need to be understood as one program and not separate entities. Remember, you goal is to adopt a proactive lifestyle for brain health that increases your brain reserve through exposure to the complex and novel. As with any lifestyle program, the journey can be difficult and perhaps humbling. There is no easy or quick answer. Your brain health program is a lifelong journey towards wholeness and will require constant personal review and change. While this program is not easy, the goal of a healthier and more challenged brain is worthwhile. I have found that spending time inspecting and reviewing my own behavior and making an effort to adopt healthy change in my lifestyle can be fun.

Getting Started and Taking Inventory

The first step for your brain health program is to understand the five critical parts of the program (*socialization, physical activity, mental stimulation, spirituality, nutrition*). Also, you must appreciate your brain as a highly dynamic system that will react to the types of input you feed it. From this perspective, you can appreciate how much control you have regarding the potential health of your brain. You may finally begin to focus on the greatest system ever designed in the history of the universe, your brain!

It is helpful to review your current lifestyle to better understand the positive and negative aspects for your brain health. You will find the **Brain Health Survey** in the appendix of this text. Derive your *Baseline Score* for the Inventory prior to starting your Lifestyle Program. It is important to be honest and to understand this is simply a guide to give you an idea of where your *Baseline Brain Health Lifestyle* is. Do not be alarmed if you give your current lifestyle a low grade. You have not been educated by society about the importance of your brain and you have not been informed about brain health. That is about to change!

Content of Your Brain Health Lifestyle Program

You have taken the time to learn about your brain and how capable it is at every age. You know your brain reacts favorably to enriched environments that promote the novel and complex. **This includes growth of new brain cells and an increase in your brain reserve.** You have also taken the time to review your current lifestyle and you applied an honest grade for your brain health prior to starting your program (*Baseline Brain Health Lifestyle*). Empowered by information on your brain and an honest assessment of your current brain health lifestyle you are ready to learn what activities are believed to promote brain health. Research-based activities or behaviors are organized and presented for each of the five critical parts of your brain health lifestyle program. As you read the following section it is important that you think about why such activities promote brain health and whether you have these activities in your current lifestyle. Most importantly, what will you need to do or change to include these activities in your daily lifestyle to maximize your brain health?

Socialization and Brain Health

Human beings need to be with other human beings. We really do not have a choice regarding this fact as it has been in our DNA since the beginning of time. Socialization was one of the critical factors of the enriched environment for animals that helped to foster healthy brain development.

30

Research teaches us that humans who isolate or segregate have a higher risk of dementia than those who remain integrated in society. Dementia is a clinical term that refers to loss of general intelligence, memory deficit, loss of other thinking abilities, personality change, and functional decline. There are over 70 causes of dementia and AD is the leading cause of dementia in the United States.

Socialization and brain health might be explained by the opportunity for communication, critical thought, creativity, emotional expression including intimacy, chemical connection, touch, and recreation that arises when two or more humans interact. Personal meaning and identity might also be a result of interpersonal activity or the creation of an entity or mission "larger than oneself."

BRAIN HEALTH LIFESTYLE TIP: Stay involved in your community at every age, do not retire, and have a personally meaningful reason for getting up each day!

I had the unique opportunity to provide a brief presentation on *Brain Health in America* at the National Press Club in September, 2006 (see asaging.org). I voiced my opposition to our national policy of retirement since it contradicts nearly everything about brain health. A nation enlightened on brain health encourages active involvement across the lifespan and does not reinforce or encourage removal of oneself from society to a passive and potentially isolative environment. As I travel the nation teaching audiences about their brain I always underscore the importance of remaining involved in meaningful ways. I discourage retirement as some identify their worth and very being by their occupation! What happens psychologically when they no longer have a job, particularly in a society like ours that still has archaic policies of mandatory retirement?

Since we live in a society that still has mandatory retirement for some occupations I believe the development of hobbies beginning in early to middle life (20s to 60s) is important. A hobby represents a brain that has been challenged. Multiple hobbies reflect a robust brain with neural networks that have been nurtured. Development of hobbies is a highly important behavior and a challenge for the baby boomers (those born between 1946 and 1964). Hobby development creates an enriched environment and provides a vehicle for the brain to experience the novel and complex. What hobbies do you have and do you have interests that you have been resisting or putting off for some time? Take one such interest and get started today. You are on your way to building brain reserve!

A Practical Exercise to Promote Socialization

Every community has a variety of clubs, organizations, and formal groups that seek membership. These may be part of a local church, school, or community. While most of these memberships require volunteer time they provide the value of socialization and contribution to an ongoing enterprise. What will it take for you to explore the opportunities in your community where you can provide input and value? It starts by you first understanding what skills you have. Most Americans do not know what their real mission on the planet is. We tend to be too busy to think about such questions or to explore such issues. It is an interesting question that requires some deep thought and time. If you have discovered your true mission the opportunity exists to align what it is you are called to do with what you actually do. Happiness and productivity are typically the outcome of such alignment. You have a wonderful list of talents that probably has not been tapped. Take a few moments and prepare a list of talents you think you possess. It does not matter if you have expressed them yet. These talents are most likely not related to your occupation or job description and they probably represent those things that you would like to pursue "if I only had the time." Once you have made your list of talents or skills begin to relate them to the list of organizations or clubs in your community. Do you notice any potential alignments where your talents can increase the value of the particular organization or club? You might even have the entrepreneurial spirit to begin your own club, group or business using your talents to lead the way! The point of this exercise is to realize that socialization is important to brain health, that identifying opportunities for socialization in your community and combining that with your own innate talents can foster an enriched environment for your brain health.

Brain Health Tip: Develop hobbies, identify your own innate talents and align them with ongoing groups or organizations in your community.

PHYSICAL ACTIVITY AND BRAIN HEALTH

Animals that ran on a wheel generated new brain cells in studies conducted in the late 1950s. This research underscores the importance of physical activity to animal brain health. The same relationship between physical activity and brain health appears to be true for humans. It is important to understand why physical activity relates to brain health. Every time your heart beats 25% of the blood and nutrients from that one heart beat goes directly to your brain. We have known for some time that physical exercise is critical to cardiac health. Research is now beginning to underscore a similar value for physical exercise to brain health! Indeed, a 2006 study by Colcombe and colleagues found that as little as three hours a week of brisk walking (aerobic exercise) increases blood flow to the brain and may trigger neurochemical changes that increase production of new brain cells. The regions of the brain most affected by the aerobic exercise included the frontal lobes (important for complex thinking, reasoning, and attention) and the corpus collosum (the bundle of white matter that bridges the two sides of the brain). This study is important for several reasons:

1. The results further support brain plasticity and new brain cell development in humans.
2. The study was conducted on persons aged 60-79 indicating brain health can occur in later life. This is consistent with animal brain research showing positive effects at advanced ages. Remember I do not believe in a critical period of brain development unless it is defined as life!
3. This may be the first study to demonstrate healthy structural changes in the human brain with physical activity; a finding we know exists for animals.
4. We know a relationship exists between physical changes in the brain (positive and negative) and functional or cognitive ability.

I have no doubt that research will further support the relationship between physical activity and brain health. This relationship likely exists at all ages and with healthy and diseased brains. Do not underestimate the power of blood flow and oxygen to the brain. Other research suggests walking on a daily basis or at least several times a week can reduce the risk of dementia. This finding again supports the relationship between physical activity and reduction in the risk of brain disease. Reduction in the risk of dementia is what I call brain health. Interestingly, there appears to be a dosing effect; the more you walk during the week the more positive effect for the brain. I have learned that most Americans know they should be walking daily and that they can even specify the need to walk about 10,000 steps daily. This tells me that our nation has done a good job educating the consumer. Unfortunately, education does not necessarily translate into action or behavior. I read recently that only about 35% of our nation is involved in a formal and consistent exercise program! As one interested in behavior, I always want to provide a personal touch to behavior and behavior change. I can tell you to walk on a daily basis and to try and take 10,000 steps daily. However, what are the chances of you actually doing it?

My recommendation to my audiences interested in brain health is to purchase a pedometer. You can purchase a pedometer at any local shopping mall or sports store. You will derive tremendous value for your $15.00 purchase as the pedometer will keep track of your daily steps and it will also remind you to walk. I always recommend you buy one for a loved one in your family, it makes a great birthday present. Have some fun with it!

Brain Health Tip: Get physically active with at least three hours of aerobic exercise a week and walk for distance three to five times per week. It is recommended that we all walk around 10,000 steps daily! Purchase a pedometer.

You now have been taught that aerobic exercise and walking on a daily basis have physical and functional benefit to your brain. You know why physical activity helps to increase brain health (25% of blood output from each heartbeat) and you have been taught a practical tip on purchasing a pedometer to help change your behavior. You will be pleased to learn that there are other physical activities you can enjoy that relate to reduced risk of dementia. The interesting thing about these activities is that you will need to use both sides of your body, a brain boosting exercise. I am often amused by the fact that most of us not only have a dominant side, but we have almost completely neglected our non-dominant side. It is important to understand that each side of your body is controlled by the opposite side of the brain. As such, most of us have essentially ignored one half of our brain! My message to audiences across the nation interested in brain health is to start on the road to becoming ambidextrous; an ambidextrous brain is a healthier brain.

Other brain health promoting physical activities include dance, particularly the tango as it has been shown to reduce the risk of dementia. I am not sure we have the ability to specify how much dance or how often we should dance yet, but this behavior appears to be healthy for the brain. Gardening and knitting are two activities that also relate to reduced risk of dementia. Once again, notice that dance, gardening, and knitting demand use of both sides of the body. In thinking about how knitting and gardening might lead to brain health it is useful to consider what the brain is asked to do with these activities. For example, with gardening your brain will be asked to plan into the future, engage in visuospatial function (where do you plant the corn relative to the carrots?), and visuomotor skill. This says nothing about the stress reduction effect gardening might offer. We Americans need to learn that a health effect can be derived by things other than pills, liquids, and shots!

Brain Health Tip: Consider taking dance lessons, start a garden, and learn how to knit.

There are some general rules that appear to be useful regarding physical activity and brain health:

1. Cardiovascular health is important to brain health. The more you can increase the strength of your heart and the output of blood from the heart through physical activities the healthier your brain will probably be.
2. Focus your behavioral change on those physical activities research has found to be important to brain health.
3. Begin to develop an ambidextrous brain by using your non-dominant body half more often. Consider writing with your non-dominant hand several minutes every day. You will be amazed as your practice leads to increased comfort and legibility (brain reserve is being built).

Mental Stimulation and Brain Health

Because your brain is the single greatest information processing system in the universe it is not surprising that many focus on the mental stimulation factor in brain health. Indeed, there are numerous computer-based products being sold to the consumer that aim to provide memory and other cognitive training exercises. You can challenge yourself with these mental exercises on a daily basis with the hope of improving your different cognitive or thinking abilities. You can use the software on your own computer or gain access to an internet site where you can complete your mental workout. A 2006 study by Willis and colleagues is the first to document long term positive effects of cognitive training on everyday function in older adults. We will likely continue to see new businesses emerging around the desire of improving the mental aspects of the brain. This represents another example of a cultural shift towards brain health!

At the same time new businesses are developing, research is providing us with information on what mentally stimulating lifestyle activities help to promote brain health or reduce risk of dementia by building brain reserve. Language appears to be critical regarding brain development and sophistication of the language system in young adulthood might actually be predictive of brain health in late life. Dr. Snowdon who leads the Nun Study has found that the number of ideas expressed in a diary written by 21 year-old females predicted percentage of tangles in the brain (marker of AD) nearly 60 years later. Snowdon proposed that language sophistication in early life might mark a well-developed brain resistant to neurodegenerative changes later in life. In contrast, a language system not well developed in early life may mark a vulnerable brain, at risk for neurodegenerative changes in later life. This work is supported by other studies that report a relationship between IQ in early life and risk of dementia such as AD in later life. Young boys who fought in WW-II took an IQ test prior to their enlistment. Their scores on the IQ test at the age of 18 have been found to correlate with presence of AD in later life. The higher the IQ at age 18 the lower the risk of AD and vice versa. Other research in Scotland has found a relationship between mental state scores at age 7 and cognitive integrity in the 70s. These findings underscore the point made earlier in this text about the need to be proactive and treat brain health as a lifespan issue.

There is some interesting work done on sign language in infants prior their neurological ability to speak. Infants can learn about 20 signs prior to being able to speak orally. When the infants exposed to sign language are followed they have greater articulation abilities and their IQ is higher by the 2nd grade relative to controls. As we learned earlier, higher IQ early in life relates to reduced risk of dementia later in life. Once again interventions early in life that enhance IQ and develop the language system appear to be examples of proactive brain health. The good news is we know IQ can be increased with good nutrition, a loving environment, breast feeding, and sign language. How many of these are in your health care plan? Every baby wellness program or head start program should include each of these brain health behaviors!

Brain Health Tip: Develop your language system, learn a new language, read and write daily, and expose your brain (particularly your baby's) to sign language.

Research has taught us that board game playing helps to reduce the risk of dementia. You probably never thought of your family game of Scrabble or Monopoly as a brain health workout. Other games such as poker, bridge, Sudoku, and the cross word puzzle probably have brain health promoting effects so long as they are "novel and complex." Once any activity becomes "rote and passive" to you the positive brain health effects have been reduced.

Reading and writing on a daily basis is good for your brain. These activities help with new learning thereby involving the hippocampus. The more you stimulate and massage your hippocampi the better. Try to read new material or new topics and write with the intent of expressing ideas. Remember; try to write with your non-dominant hand a few minutes a day. Reading and speaking to the baby developing in the womb may have neurological benefit to the baby. Mom and Dad, you are encouraged to get involved in shaping your baby's brain!

Lifelong learning programs are now part of the social norm with many universities across the nation sponsoring such programs. I have had the pleasure of learning about the value and fun of Elderhostel and Osher Lifelong Learning programs. Hundreds of thousands of older adults are enrolling in university classroom work as part of their "retirement." What used to be the beach or the golf course is now a book and classroom! I have spoken for many years about how learning is a health promoting entity no different than a medication. Learning involves structural, chemical, and functional changes in your brain that can be health promoting. Indeed research indicates education is a major factor contributing to longevity and health. The actual event of learning something new involves the laying down of a new neural network that was not there before. With continued learning, the brain develops a rich network of neural associations we refer to as brain reserve. It is this brain reserve that helps to delay onset of neurodegenerative disorders such as AD. It is for this reason that I have argued lifelong learning programs should be part of every health care payer system including Medicare!

Lifelong learning means lifelong and does not infer a starting point in late life. I believe every elementary school in this nation should be mandated to teach the basics of the brain to American children. In order to be proactive we need to begin very early in life. Our children will more likely care for their brains if they understand this wonderful part of their being. The earlier the education occurs the earlier a proactive lifestyle for brain health can be started. As we learned earlier, the types of environments we expose our brains to early in life relate to the health of our brains later in life. In this regard, I am pleased to know that teachers and neuroscientists are working together to merge the lesson plan and brain scan!

Brain Health Tip: Enroll in a lifelong learning program in your community or at your local University. Encourage your local school board to integrate curriculum on the basics of the human brain within the elementary school—be proactive!

Classic music has been found to have a relationship to learning in children. It is not uncommon to observe classic music being played in some classrooms during study period or perhaps even during a test. Study time at home can be enhanced with background classic music. Once again, some work indicates classic music played for the baby developing in the womb has neurological benefit. You are also encouraged to try and learn to play a musical instrument. It is true that learning to play a musical instrument is harder as you age, but your brain can learn an instrument at any age. Do not be afraid to develop that dormant part of your brain!

Brain Health Tip: Start to play those wonderful board games again, learn a musical instrument, and tune in to the classic radio station.

Travel has been shown to reduce the risk of dementia, or better said, to increase brain health. Consider how this behavior might be brain health promoting. You already know that the best environment for your brain is the complex and novel. When you travel away from home you are leaving a familiar surrounding and exposing your brain to a novel and complex environment. As a result, you will use your cortex to navigate and you will probably find it exciting and maybe frustrating at times. Interestingly, as you stay in that new environment you will become more familiar and comfortable. The novel and complex has become rote and passive. Everyday you travel to and from work and home and essentially do not use your cortex. Your subcortex has the mental maps of your home and neighborhood and the processing tends to be rote or subconscious. New environments are more brain health promoting. The other nice thing about travel is that you will meet new people who contribute to your enriched environment.

Brain Health Tip: Try and take a trip or two this year to a new surrounding and enjoy the brain health benefits!

Spirituality and Brain Health

I have noticed that Americans are a bit timid when talking about spirituality. I often have an audience member come up to me after my talk and whisper their thanks for my speaking about spirituality. It feels like we are doing something wrong! I am not sure how our nation got to this point, but there will be no fear in this text to discuss an important health promoting behavior. Spirituality has many meanings and it may mean something different to you than me. This section refers to spirituality as one means of turning inward to a peaceful existence and to remove oneself from the hurried society that is America. In this regard I employ prayer, meditation, and relaxation procedures as three tangible examples of spirituality.

Animal research has found that rodents raised in an environment that is too stimulating demonstrate slowed brain development. In addition, animals exposed to environments that are highly stressful and where they have little control demonstrate structural damage in their hippocampus and evince memory problems. The point of this animal research is that we humans should take pause and examine how fast we are moving on a daily basis and decide if we need to slow down. Early research on the human brain exposed to life threatening stressors indicates there is similar damage to the hippocampus as is known to exist in animals. Also, humans with chronic anxiety have memory problems again supporting the negative effect of stress and uncontrolled anxiety on brain function.

Research and surveys have reported the following positive effects of prayer on health:

1. Prayer on a daily basis relates to an enhanced immune system, the system that helps you defend against colds, flu, and other illnesses.
2. Those who attend a formalized place of worship live longer and report happier and healthier lives than those who do not. Unfortunately, surveys suggest only 30% of the nation attend a formalized place of worship weekly.
3. Prayer as part of the daily routine while in the hospital relates to an earlier discharge. I would think the health care payer system would find this interesting!
4. According to a past Parade Magazine Survey, 95% of the physicians in the U.S. believe prayer is important to the well-being of their patients. I wonder if a prescription for the Our Father makes sense?

Brain Health Tip: Consider attending a formalized place of worship on a weekly basis and incorporate prayer into your daily health routine.

Meditation and relaxation procedures are also good techniques to help you slow down and to turn inward for balance and symmetry. Your brain can adapt to a chaotic world, but it will function more efficiently over a longer period of time if you provide moments of inward reflection and rest. Meditation offers one technique to achieve such inner peace. Interestingly, the brains of monks in deep meditation show changes in glucose metabolism. The brains of the monks no longer distinguish the outside world from their internal world. The saying "I became one with my world" takes on real meaning. Most Americans do not know how to meditate and part of your brain health program can include a lesson or two on meditation so you can engage in this behavior on a daily basis.

Similar to meditation, relaxation procedures that include deep breathing and progressive muscle relaxation exercises are not well known or used by Americans. Our nation tends to favor the pill over lifestyle behaviors, the quick fix over patience. Unfortunately, we tend to use band-aid approaches and we really do not fix the underlying problems or struggles of our lives. It is important to identify what part of your body is vulnerable to stress. You may experience stress in your neck, lower back, head, or stomach. By identifying what part of your body is your stress target site you can then engage in progressive muscle relaxation procedures to alleviate the stress from your target site. For example, squeeze your right hand into a fist as hard as you can. Hold the fist and pay attention to how uncomfortable the tension is in your fist. Now, slowly release your fingers extending them and notice how the tension leaves your fingers. The more relaxed feeling achieved by letting the fist go and extending your fingers is an example of how you can focus on any muscle group in your body to release stress. You can actually tighten and release muscles all over your body two to three times a day. At the end of the exercise you will notice that energy in the form of stress has left you and you will feel better!

Similarly, you may not know how to breathe correctly or to use breathing techniques to rid your body of stress. You are encouraged to engage in proper relaxation breathing exercises two to three times daily. Taking a deep inhalation through your nose using your stomach muscles and holding the breath for several seconds will result in your feeling some tension in your stomach and chest. Now, slowly release the air from your stomach and chest out your mouth in a rhythmic way. Doing this exercise several times throughout the day can help you to slow down and gain a sense of calm as you rid yourself of toxic stress.

Brain Health Tip: Enroll in a meditation class and begin to incorporate meditation into your brain health program. Employ progressive muscle relaxation and deep breathing exercises two to three times daily. Turning inward will help your brain escape temporarily the stress filled and un-enriched environments of life.

One final brain health promoting behavior you will enjoy is sleep! A staggering number of Americans have sleep disorders and it is common for Americans to respond "I am tired" when they are asked how they are doing. Sleep is actually a very active time for the brain. There are four stages of sleep and the brain requires each, particularly Rapid Eye Movement (REM) the 25% of our sleep when you dream. If you do not sleep, your brains will sleep for you and this can be fatal such as when one automatically falls asleep while driving. This is known as Narcolepsy.

Some studies indicate that your brain actually consolidates information into a well-organized and formed memory during sleep. You can appreciate why sleep is so important if it is involved in your information processing and ability to recall potentially important details. Those who do not accrue enough sleep have a higher risk of thinking problems and mood disorder such as depression. Work related accidents and motor vehicle accidents are examples of negative outcomes from poor sleep. Are you getting enough sleep? If not, why not and what are you doing about it? There are many reasons for sleep disorder including anxiety, bills, pain, interpersonal or family conflict, and medication side effects. Each of these causes can have a different solution or treatment to regain a normal sleep pattern. Remember that sleep is a learned behavior and it can be altered in many ways.

A sleep pattern can be re-learned provided consistent behavior is adhered to in the form of time to go to bed, using the bed for sleep and not reading or t.v., and not laying in bed when you are not sleeping. You can probably give yourself 20 to 25 minutes to try and get to sleep in your bed. If you cannot fall asleep after that time period, get out of the bed and leave the bedroom. You may even identify an "anxiety chair" in your house where you can go sit and worry all you want. When you are done worrying go back to your bed and try to sleep. The same 20 to 25 minute rule holds and you may need to get up several times. The point with this exercise is to condition your body and brain to sleep in the bed, not worry in the bed!

Brain Health Tip: Try and get enough sleep to feel rested in the morning. Speak to your M.D. if you have problems with your sleep to understand why and to develop a remedy.

Nutrition and Brain Health

Brain health and nutrition has become a very popular and intense area of study. Entire books are devoted to food and its effect on the brain and a new journal, Nutritional Neurosciences, recognizes this emerging specialization. This book cannot cover the entire content area of brain health and nutrition, but it is certainly included and represents a critical part of my Brain Health Lifestyle Program.

General tips regarding brain health and nutrition include the following:

1. Increase your intake of omega-3 fatty acids because your brain contains at least 60% fat.
2. Increase your intake of antioxidants to help combat free radical development.
3. Increase your intake of colored fruits and vegetables including green leafy vegetables.
4. Eat with utensils and you will likely eat healthier foods, and reduce your caloric intake.
5. Reduce your intake of red meat.
6. Eliminate trans-fatty acids from your diet and try to reduce your intake of processed foods.
7. Eat at least one meal a day with family or friends. This is a rich brain health behavior because you communicate, listen to classic music, slow down, eat with utensils, eat healthy foods, and eat less.

Because the field of nutrition and neurosciences is so specialized I have asked *Ms. Lauren Dorgant* to contribute her knowledge on the subject. Her biography is listed in the back of the book. I appreciate Lauren's work and I know you will enjoy her section on nutrition. Please take special notice of Lauren's recommendations and have fun with her sample menu for brain health! This section is to be integrated with the other four parts of my brain health lifestyle program.

INTRODUCTION TO FOOD
AND YOUR BRAIN

With all the mixed advice being passed around regarding diets, nutrition and your health—who knows who or *what* to believe! There are TV commercials, magazine ads, the infamous late night infomercials on a "new and revolutionary" diet pill or a "recently discovered" magic herb in the Swiss Alps. Then there are your friends, family members and coworkers who always seem most convincing. There is literally diet advice around every corner. Who has the best recommendation? What *are* the healthiest ways to diet? What will keep you and your body healthy for life?

Eating a well-balanced, healthy diet not only has the benefit of helping you fit into your favorite pair of jeans, but it can also help you reduce your risk of chronic age-related brain diseases such as dementia and Alzheimer's. Current research in diet and brain health has shown that nutrition plays a large part in brain development and function throughout the life cycle. There are changes you can make *now* to prolong the health of your body's most vital system, your brain.

Before starting any "diet" or taking any nutrition advice you should ask yourself one simple question, "Is this a plan I can continue to follow one day from now, one week from now and even one year from now?" If you cannot truthfully and realistically answer "yes" to these questions, then the diet is probably not very practical for you. A healthy lifestyle does require you to make changes for the betterment of your overall health. You should not think of these changes as losses, but rather as steps you can take now to improve your overall current health, reduce your risk of future ailments and generally improve your day-to-day mental health and well-being.

Your brain has nutritional needs too.

Your brain is a complex system that requires vitamins, minerals and antioxidants for daily functioning and mental sharpness. The good news: you can find these powerful vitamins, minerals and antioxidants right in the foods you eat.

There are several components of a healthy diet that aid in promoting overall brain health and function. Some of the most essential include a group of *antioxidants* like carotenoids, vitamins A, C and E, the mineral selenium and folate. Other important components that can help combat mental health decline are the *phytochemicals* and *omega-3 fatty acids*.

Antioxidants

You have probably heard that a diet rich in antioxidants can help prevent minor illnesses like colds, and reduce risk of major illnesses such as heart disease. Antioxidants may also can keep the brain operating at its peak to help reduce risk of serious conditions such as Alzheimer's. Antioxidants are powerful substances that help counteract the damaging effects of oxygen in the tissues of the body.

Antioxidants play a housekeeper's role by essentially "cleaning up" free radicals before they can cause damage to your body. Free radicals are highly reactive atoms formed when oxygen and certain molecules interact. These free radicals have an unpaired electron that can cause cell damage, eventually leading to the decline in function or even cell death. Our body's main defense against these damaging free radicals is *antioxidants*. The antioxidants include beta-carotene (and other carotenoids), Vitamins A, C and E, and the mineral Selenium.

• Carotenoids

Carotenoids are a class of pigments that give many fruits and vegetables their color and can range from yellow to orange to red or purple. Without carotenoids, for example, carrots would not be orange and tomatoes would not be red. Carotenoids function as antioxidants by helping to protect plants from harmful free radical damage. In the human body, they work to guard cells from the danger of free radicals that can be produced during metabolism, from cigarette smoke and other pollutants or even from stress. There are over 600 known carotenoids, but one of the most recognized is beta carotene.

Beta Carotene is necessary for the creation of Vitamin A by the body and is responsible for the pigment in deep orange-colored foods. *Some fruits and vegetables that are particularly rich sources of beta-carotene include*:

- carrots
- pumpkin
- salmon

- sweet potatoes
- tomatoes
- cantaloupe
- peaches
- apricots

- **Vitamin A**, also known as "retinol," can be made by the body from beta-carotene. Vitamin A helps protect orange, yellow and dark green vegetables and fruits from the sun's harmful radiation. It is also believed to have a comparable role in the human body. Vitamin A is essential for vision, cell growth, and healthy skin, teeth and bones.

Good sources of Vitamin A include:
- carrot juice
- sweet potato with peel
- pumpkin
- spinach
- collard greens
- kale
- beets

- **Vitamin C,** also known as "ascorbic acid," is another antioxidant that helps to protect from free radical damage. Getting enough Vitamin C is a key to keeping your immune system healthy and protecting you from the common cold and other illnesses. Your body is incapable of producing this necessary vitamin; therefore, it is crucial that you acquire it daily from the diet. Vitamin C is also a primary ingredient in the formation of collagen, the glue that holds your cells together. It is used to form the skin layer that acts as a natural barrier during the healing process of wounds and cuts.

Excellent sources of Vitamin C include the citrus fruits. Some examples are:

- oranges
- lemons
- limes
- grapefruit

Other good sources of Vitamin C include:

- green peppers
- broccoli
- green leafy vegetables
- strawberries
- blueberries
- raw cabbage
- tomatoes

- **Vitamin E**

Vitamin E is used by the body to help protect the nervous system and the retinas of the eye, to help lower your risk for heart attacks and heart disease, and to protect you from irregular blood clotting that can essentially prevent strokes. It may also be helpful in lowering your risk for certain kinds of cancer; particularly melanoma, because it works to stop skin cancer cell growth. Vitamin E also works with vitamin A to protect the lungs against pollutants in the air, may lessen cellular aging and guards immune system function. More importantly, Vitamin E can reduce your risk of neurodegenerative diseases like Alzheimer's by protecting the brain cells from damage.

Good sources of Vitamin E include:
- nuts
- seeds
- whole grains
- green leafy vegetables
- wheat germ
- canola oil and other vegetable oils
- fish-liver oil

• Selenium

The mineral Selenium is another antioxidant that helps prevent free radical damage to protect your brain against unhealthy aging. It also can help with the prevention of dangerous blood clots including "brain attacks" (strokes). Selenium is found primarily in nuts and seeds, but can be found in other foods as well.
Good sources of selenium include:
- Brazil nuts
- canned tuna
- shellfish
- lean cuts of beef, turkey & chicken
- enriched noodles
- oatmeal and other grains
- cottage cheese
- garlic
- sesame seeds

• Folate

Also known as folic acid, folate is one of the B vitamins that have been proven to be beneficial for brain health.

In one study, the risk of the development of Alzheimer's disease was reduced by 55% by eating the recommended daily allowance of folate[1]. One explanation for this finding is that elevated homocysteine levels are known to cause damage to the cells of the brain. Getting an adequate amount of folate helps to lower homocysteine levels in the blood that can in turn reduce the risk for Alzheimer's.

Good sources of folate include:
- fortified breakfast cereals
- chickpeas
- asparagus
- spinach
- black, kidney & lima beans
- Brussels sprouts
- oranges
- broccoli

Photochemicals

A phytochemical is any nutrient or chemical derived from a plant source that is not considered to be a necessity for normal functioning of the body, but can have beneficial effects on health. They are found primarily in fruits and vegetables and appear to promote health in several ways. They may slow the aging process and also reduce your risk for disease. *Some of the phytochemicals beneficial to your health include lycopene, reservatrol and the flavonoids.*

• Lycopene
Found in tomatoes and tomato products, pink grapefruit and watermelon, lycopene serves as an antioxidant that

may aid in the reduction of heart disease and even the prevention of prostate cancer. Lycopene can also help to ward off the effects of free radicals on the brain.

• Reservatrol

Found in red grapes, wine and peanuts, reservatrol may help reduce your risk of heart disease and cancer. Because wine contains reservatrol, it is known to be beneficial for cardiac health when consumed in small amounts. This reservatrol in wine can also be beneficial for brain function by perhaps extending the life of the brain cells[2]. This occurs by stimulation of an enzyme which interacts with proteins that regulate reactions to stressors and longevity. Recommendations for wine intake are controversial, however, one glass (4 to 6 oz) of wine per day for women and 1-2 for men is generally considered sufficient. Those predisposed to alcohol addiction or breast cancer and those told by their physicians not to consume alcohol should listen to their physician.

• Flavonoids

Flavonoids are organic compounds found in fruits, vegetables and some beverages that, according to recent studies, may be beneficial by acting as antioxidants[3]. Certain flavonoids, like those found in beer, have been shown to have surprisingly powerful antioxidant effects; some exceeding the flavonoids found in soy, tea and even red wine. Beer, like wine or any alcoholic beverages, should be consumed in moderation (see advice above). There are over 4,000 known flavonoids. *Some good sources of flavonoids include*:

- vegetable and fruit skins
- soy
- tea
- citrus fruits
- onions
- hops & beer
- red wine

Anthocyanins

Anthocyanins are one of the most *visible* flavonoids. Anthocyanin pigments can range in color from deep red to purple or blue. This compound is responsible, for example, for making blueberries blue. Anthocyanins are found in flowers and fruits, but are also present in roots, leaves, seeds and stems, along with other parts of plants. Together with the carotenoids, these two antioxidant-like compounds are responsible for the classic-colored tree leaves of the autumn season. Anthocyanins are also known for their antioxidant-like effects of cleaning up free radicals.

Some foods that contain anthocyanins include:
- blueberries
- cranberries
- strawberries
- blackberries
- cherries
- kiwi
- plums
- eggplant

An added benefit of these foods is that all can help to prevent urinary tract infections! Fresh berries may be expensive if out of season, so a comparable and healthy substitute includes frozen berries.

The Truth About...Dark Chocolate!

Along with being a very savory treat, dark chocolate also contains flavonoids. However, there are a few things you should know before you go on your next mid-afternoon chocolate binge! Chocolate is a food that is very high in calories, saturated fat and sugar. Interestingly, dark chocolate may benefit your health — only when *occasionally* eaten in *moderate* amounts. The benefit comes from the cocoa that is derived from the "cacao" plant, which is known to be rich in flavonoids.

According to a recent study[4], dark chocolate rich in flavonoids may help prevent bad cholesterol (LDL) from causing plaque to buildup in the arteries of the heart. Another study[5] showed that these flavonoids could possibly lower blood pressure in persons with hypertension. Both benefits could possibly help prevent strokes in persons with high cholesterol or high blood pressure. For the occasional dark chocolate indulgence, take your time and *enjoy* the creamy texture and rich flavor of the chocolate—you may realize that one square is just enough to satisfy your craving.

So which foods have the most antioxidant power?

You may be interested in knowing what foods have the best antioxidant power for my diet and my health? In 2004, researchers at the United States Department of Agriculture conducted their largest analysis of 100 commonly eaten foods that contain the largest concentrations of antioxidants per serving. The results of the study confirm the long-time belief that fruits and vegetables are an essential part of general health and wellness. *Listed below are some of the foods that contained the highest levels of antioxidants according to the USDA research[6].*

Fruits	**Nuts**
Cranberries	Pecans
Blueberries	Walnuts
Blackberries	Hazelnuts
Black plums	Pistachios

Vegetables	**Spices**
Pinto and kidney beans	Ground cloves
Artichokes	Ground cinnamon
Black-eyed peas	Dried oregano
Red cabbage	Turmeric

Omega-3-fatty acids

Fish is another food that can help you ensure healthy function of the cells of the brain because it is rich in a substance known as omega-3 fatty acids. Because our bodies do not naturally produce Omega-3 fatty acids, we are reliant on the diet to provide them. Fish also does not have the high saturated fat content other fatty meat products have.

Fish especially rich in the omega-3 fatty acids include:
- mackerel
- lake trout
- herring

- sardines
- albacore tuna
- salmon

Recall that your brain is comprised of at least 60% fat and the fatty or lipid part of your brain helps to transmit information rapidly across your neural networks. Consumption of Omega-3 fatty acids is thought to help maintain proper fat in your brain and to facilitate information processing. Indeed, some research demonstrates a relationship between several ounces of salmon a week and reduction in the risk of dementia.

OTHER LIFESTYLE FACTORS: THE FACTORS OF LIFE

Other lifestyle factors like obesity, high blood pressure or cholesterol levels and inadequate exercise may also contribute to dementia.

Obesity

Being overweight or obese has been known to cause many health-related illnesses such as heart disease, diabetes, high blood pressure, among countless others. Can being overweight or obese also lead to a decline in brain function? The answer is yes!

Being overweight or obese during mid-life has been shown to increase the risk for decline in brain function later in life, according to scientific research. A recent publication[7] discovered that compared to people of normal weight, those who are overweight or obese in their 40s have a much greater risk of developing of Alzheimer's disease.

This study included 9,000 participants between 40 and 45 years of age who were deemed overweight or obese by way of skin-fold fat measurements at the beginning of the trial. After follow-ups were conducted (up to 30 years for some participants), 221 cases of Alzheimer's disease were diagnosed. Conclusions from the research show that participants in their 40s with the highest skin-fold fat measurements were about three times more likely to develop the disease than those with the smallest skin-fold fat measurements. The research also concluded that those who had the largest arm measurements were 2? times more likely to develop Alzheimer's disease than those in the group with the smallest skin-fold fat measurements. This decade-long research-based evidence really emphasizes that being overweight or obese does play a role in late-life brain functionality. Although there is no clear evidence of the exact correlation between obesity and dementia, researchers believe several mechanisms explain the link. Some include, fat regulation hormones leptin and adiponectin, co-morbid medical conditions, and inflammatory response proteins called cytokines. These results further stress the role of diet and nutrition as key factors in maintaining a healthy weight and promoting life-long brain health.

Your Ideal Body Weight

Are you at your ideal body weight? Are you at risk for developing dementia or even Alzheimer's later in life? An easy way to figure out your own *ideal* weight is through the following formula:

Ideal Body Weight (**IBW**) * =

If you are male:

106 lbs for 5 feet tall. Add 6 lbs for every inch over 5 feet.

Ex: Dustin is 5'10" tall.

Therefore his *Ideal Body Weight* would be:

106 + (6 lbs x10")

106 + 60

= 166 lbs

63

If you are female:
100 lbs for 5 feet tall. Add 5 lbs for every inch over 5 feet.
Ex: Sarah is 5'5" tall.
Therefore her *Ideal Body Weight* would be:
100 + (5 lbs x 5")
100 + 25
= 125 lbs

Figure out YOUR IBW!**

Your height = _____

If male: 106 + (6lbs x _____)
Your IBW = _____#

If female: 100 + (5lbs x _____)
Your IBW = _____#

---

* *Note: If you are less than 5 feet tall, subtract 2.5 lbs per inch less than 5 feet.*

** *The IBW formula is not for everyone. It is for the average adult between the ages of 20 and 65 who wants to determine their desirable body weight range. The IBW is not for pregnant or lactating women or for children. If you are concerned about your weight, please consult your health care provider.*

If you are within 10% (about 10-15 pounds) of this *Ideal Body Weight*, you are in a healthy weight range. If you weigh more than 10% of your IBW, then you would be classified as overweight for your height. If you weight more than 30% of your IBW, then you would then be classified as obese. Being overweight or obese is a risk factor for many serious conditions and weight reduction should be seriously considered for your overall health.

Blood pressure

The amount of sodium you take in through the foods you eat can directly affect your blood pressure. High blood pressure can lead to a number of health conditions like heart disease or kidney disease. High blood pressure can also influence brain health because of increased risk of strokes. Eating too much sodium-containing salt is one of the primary ways your blood pressure increases.

Sodium, that is most commonly found in table salt, is also found in extremely high amounts in food items that contain preservatives. Preservatives are used to keep foods looking and tasting fresh for any set period of time. Some of the items that contain high amounts of salt and/or preservatives include canned vegetables and soups, frozen microwaveable dinners and smoked or processed meats like hot dogs, sausages and lunch meats. Following a lower-sodium diet can be the key to helping relieve high blood pressure.

A Nutrition Facts Label Example

If you were to look at the "Nutrition Facts" label on the back of any food item, an ideal amount of sodium to look for would be 140 milligrams or less per serving. This would mean that the particular item would be considered "low-sodium" and contains minimal amounts of salt and other sodium-containing preservatives.

See for yourself! Check out the *Nutrition Facts* label below. When reading a label, the first thing you should always check is the serving size. The serving size will differ from item to item, thus, you will need to look at this for each food. On this particular *Nutrition Facts* label, the serving size is "1 cup." If you scan down to the sodium content, you will find that this particular item contains 660 milligrams of sodium per serving. So, for every 1 cup of this item, this means you will take in nearly 5 times what is recommended per serving for sodium intake! If the item contained less than 140 milligrams per serving, then it would be considered a "low-sodium" item and could be labeled as such.

Nutrition Facts

Serving Size 1 cup (228g)
Servings Per Container 2

Amount Per Serving

Calories 260   Calories from Fat 120

% Daily Value*

Total Fat 13g	**20%**
Saturated Fat 5g	**25%**
Trans Fat 2g	
Cholesterol 30mg	**10%**
Sodium 660mg	**28%**
Total Carbohydrate 31g	**10%**
Dietary Fiber 0g	**0%**
Sugars 5g	
Protein 5g	

Vitamin A 4%	•	Vitamin C 2%	
Calcium 15%	•	Iron 4%	

* Percent Daily Values are based on a 2,000 calorie diet.
Your Daily Values may be higher or lower depending on
your calorie needs:

		Calories:	2,000	2,500
Total Fat	Less than		65g	80g
Sat Fat	Less than		20g	25g
Cholesterol	Less than		300mg	300mg
Sodium	Less than		2,400mg	2,400mg
Total Carbohydrate			300g	375g
Dietary Fiber			25g	30g

Calories per gram:
Fat 9   •   Carbohydrate 4   •   Protein 4

Cholesterol

High blood cholesterol levels can lead to heart conditions and can also contribute to a decline in brain health. Cholesterol is a fatty substance closely related to the development of blocked blood vessels. Cholesterol comes from two sources: it is naturally produced by the body and it can come from the foods you eat.

Why does cholesterol influence brain health? Simply stated, the answer is high cholesterol causes an increase in buildup on the blood vessel walls. When this "plaque" builds up, there is less room for the blood to flow through your blood vessels which leads to an increased risk of clots that can cause blockages to the heart (heart attacks) or to the brain (strokes). Remember, your brain demands 25% of the blood from each heartbeat.

Lowering the amount of cholesterol you eat can aid in the prevention of these chronic illnesses. Cholesterol is only found in foods from animal products. Some examples would be butter, milk, cheese, any meats, lard and others.

Take another look at the Nutrition Facts Label. If you wanted to purchase foods low in cholesterol, you would simply look for items with 20 milligrams or less per serving. For this particular food item, each cup contains 30 milligrams of cholesterol, which does *not* make it a "low cholesterol" food.

Physical activity

Physical activity is another key component of increased brain function because of the increased blood flow to the brain areas and the chemical response of the body during and after exercise. Exercise helps to release the "feel-good" hormone *Endorphin*. This hormone has a positive effect on the body by helping to lower stress levels and improving self-esteem. Read more about this topic in the physical activity chapter of this book.

"FOOD FOR THOUGHT"

After reading this section on nutrition and brain health, you might have noted an overall theme: eating more fruits and vegetables relates to brain health! The Dietary Guidelines currently recommend that most Americans should aim for "5-a-day"— about 2 cups of fruit and 2 cups of vegetables per day for overall health. Seems simple enough, right? But, are *you* going to make the nutritional changes to improve your own brain health? Lifestyle changes are important and extremely *necessary* to enhance brain health and prevent chronic illnesses. Start now and reap the benefits of improved overall brain function.

References (Nutrition Section)

1. Corrada MM, Kawas CH, Hallfrisch J, et al. Reduced risk of Alzheimer's disease with high folate intake: The Baltimore longitudinal study of aging. Alzheimer's & Dementia 2005;1:11-18.
2. Howitz KT, Bitterman KJ, Bohen HY, et al. Small molecule activators of sirtuins extend Saccharomyces cerevisiae lifespan. Nature 2003; 425:191-196.
3. Buhler DR, Miranda C. Antioxidant activities of flavonoids. Department of Environmental and Molecular Toxicology: The Linus Pauling Institute at Oregon State University. 2000 Nov. Available at:

http://lpi.oregonstate.edu/f-w00/flavonoid.html. Accessed 2006 Aug 2.

4. Engler MB, Engler MM, Chen CY, et al. Flavonoid-rich dark chocolate improves endothelial function and increases plasma epicatechin concentration in healthy adults. J Amer College of Nutr 2004;23(3):197-204.

5. Grassi D, Necozione S, Lippi C, et al. Cocoa reduces blood pressure and insulin resistance and improves endothelium-dependent vasodilation in hypertensives. Hypertension: J Amer Heart Assoc 2005;46:398.

6. Wu X, Beecher GR, Holden JM, et al. Lipophilic and hydrophilic antioxidant capacities of common foods in the United States. J Agric Food Chem 2004;52(12):4026-4037.

7. Whitmer RA, Yaffe K. Obesity and dementia: lifecourse evidence and mechanisms. Aging Health 2006;2:571-578.

Additional Resources (nutrition section)

- American Dietetic Association *www.eatright.org*
- 5-a-day organization *www.5aday.org*
- United States Department of Agriculture *www.usda.gov*
- American Heart Association *www.americanheart.org*
- Dietary Guidelines *www.health.gov/dietaryguidelines*
- ADA "Evidence Supports Good Nutrition For Active Healthy Aging" *www.eatright.org/cps/rde/xchg/ada/hs.xsl/career_1693_EN U_HTML.htm*

SUMMARY

Congratulations on taking the time to learn about your brain, the most magnificent part of you. I hope this book helped to educate you on the basics of your brain and the real power you have in shaping the health of your brain. It truly is a great time to be alive if you are interested in the human brain. We have learned so much in the past decade and I believe we are going to continue learning that the human brain has abilities we cannot even imagine.

I wrote this book to continue my mission of educating the general public about the human brain. My hope is that readers of this book will begin to better appreciate the greatness of their brain and begin to dedicate time and effort towards their own brain health. Though you may take it for granted, your life story is vital to your very being and there is good reason to begin your proactive brain health journey. Surely you have much to share with your next generation of little ones!

I will continue to care for those who suffer terrible diseases such as AD and other dementias. I will also continue my work educating the public about their brain in the hope of promoting brain health for everyone. It is true that most of us do not have dementia. It is also true that we can engage in a brain health lifestyle that will hopefully limit our risk. While we have no cure or prevention at this time, we certainly can get busy shaping our own brain in a healthy way.

I encourage all of you to become educated and to be proactive towards your own brain health. Engage in the novel and complex and expose your brain to daily environments that are enriched. Review your current lifestyle and make the necessary changes to increase your brain health using my proposed brain health lifestyle. Do not consider your age as it really is not important. Your brain will thank you for the stimulation. In the end, your proactive brain health lifestyle may actually help you maintain your life story and your little ones will thank you!

BRAIN HEALTH RESOURCES

The following resources may be helpful to your Brain Health Lifestyle.

American Society on Aging *(www.asaging.org).*

AARP *(www.aarp.com).*

www.babysigns.com.

Billings, L. M., Green, K. N., McGaugh, J. L., & LaFerla, F. M. (2007). Learning decreases AB*56 and Tau pathology and ameliorates behavioral decline in 3xTg- AD mice. *The Journal of Neuroscience,* 27, 751-761.

Carper, J. (2000). *Your miracle brain.* New York: Quill.

Colcombe, S. J., et al. (2006). Aerobic exercise training increases brain volume in aging humans. *The Journal of Gerontology: Medical Sciences, 61,* 1116-1170.

Diamond, M. C., & Hopson, J. (1999). *Magic trees of the mind.* New York: Plume.

Kotulak, R. (1997). *Inside the brain: Revolutionary discoveries of how the mind works.* Kansas City, MO: Anreas and McMeely.

Nussbaum, P. D. (2005). *Love your Brain: A Lifestyle Guide to Brain Health Across Your Lifespan.* MetLife, Ct.

Nussbaum, P. D. (2003). *Brain Health and Wellness.* Word Association Publishing: Tarentum, Pa.

Willis, S. L., et al. (2006). Long term effects of cognitive training on everyday functional outcomes in older adults. *Journal of American Medical Association,* 296, 2805-2814.

Wilson, R. S. et al. (2007). Loneliness and risk of Alzheimer's Disease. *Archives of General Psychiatry,* 64 234-240.

www.paulnussbaum.com
www.elderhostel.com
www.osherfoundation.org
www.maturemarketinstitute@metlife.com
www.emeritus.com
www.positscience.com
www.dakim.com
www.brainacuity.com
www.fda.gov (U.S. Food and Drug Administration)
www.USDA.gov (U.S. Department of Agriculture)
www.happyneuron.com
www.cdc.gov (U.S. Center for Disease Control)
www.nih.gov (U.S. National Institute for Health)
www.memoryzine.com
www.Nunstudy.com

APPENDIX ONE

Your Personal Brain Health Survey

Complete your Brain Health Survey to learn more about your own brain health!! Results are not scientific and are meant to help guide your brain health lifestyle. Your brain health profile is comprised of five major areas:

Physical
Mental
Social
Spiritual
Nutrition

The following survey uses research-based information to propose a brain healthy lifestyle. The survey is to be completed prior to starting your brain health program (*Baseline Score*) and to be repeated every three months to document your progress.

Do not be concerned if you score poorly at first. This is probably the first time you have considered your own brain health! You will notice improvement if you remain loyal to your brain health lifestyle.

Physical Domain

Circle the response that best describes your behavior over the past three months.

1. I walk 10,000 steps daily. 5 points

   I walk between 5,000 and 10,000
   steps daily. 3 points

   I do not walk. 0 points

2. I engage in aerobic exercise three
   hours a week. 5 points

   I engage in aerobic exercise one
   hour a week. 3 points

   I do not engage in aerobic exercise. 0 points

3. I garden more than one time a week
   during season. 5 points

   I garden one time a week during season. 3 points

   I do not garden. 0 points

4. I dance more than one time a week. 5 points

   I dance one time a week. 3 points

   I do not dance. 0 points

5. I knit more than one time a week.   5 points

   I knit one time a week.   3 points

   I do not knit.   0 points.

Physical Domain Total Points   _____/25

Mental Stimulation Domain

Circle the response that best describes your behavior during the past three months.

1. I read more than the news on a daily basis.   5 points

   I read one new book a month.   3 points

   I do not read.   0 points

2. I am fluent in more than one language.   5 points

   I am learning a new language including
   American Sign Language.   3 points

   I am not learning a new language.   0 points.

3. I handwrite on a daily basis.   5 points

    I handwrite once a week.   3 points

    I do not handwrite.   0 points

4. I travel to new places one time a week. 5 points

    I travel to new places one time a month. 3 points

    I do not travel to new places.   0 points

5. I play a musical instrument.   5 points

    I am learning to play a new musical
    instrument.   3 points

    I do not play a musical instrument.   0 points

6. I listen to classic music on a daily basis. 5 points

    I listen to classic music once a week. 3 points

    I do not listen to classic music.   0 points

7. I play board games or other cognitive
   games daily.   5 points

   I play board games or other
   cognitive games once weekly.   3 points

   I do not play board games or
   cognitive games.   0 points.

Mental Stimulation Total Points   _____/35

Social Domain

Circle the response that best describes your behavior during the past three months.

1. I eat one meal with my family/friends
   every day.   5 points

   I eat one meal with my family/friends
   weekly.   3 points

   I do not eat meals with anyone.   0 points

2. I have joined two or more new groups
   this year.   5 points

   I have joined one new group this year.   3 points

I have not joined any new group the
past year.   0 points

3. I have started more than one hobby in
   the past year.   5 points

   I have started one new hobby in the
   past year.   3 points

   I have not started a new hobby in the
   past year.   0 Points

4. I speak to family or friends every day.   5 points

   I speak to family or friends three times
   a week   3 points

   I speak to family or friends less than
   once weekly.   0 points

5. I engage in personally meaningful
   activity daily.   5 points

   I engage in personally meaningful activity
   one time a week.   3 points

   I do not engage in any personally
   meaningful activity.   0 Points

Social Domain Total Points   _____/25

Spiritual Domain

Circle the response that best describes your behavior during the past three months.

1. I pray on a daily basis.   5 points

    I pray one time a week.   3 points

    I do not pray.   0 points

2. I meditate on a daily basis.   5 points

    I meditate one time a week.   3 points

    I do not meditate.   0 points

3. I engage in relaxation procedures daily. 5 points

    I engage in relaxation procedures one
    time a week.   3 points

    I do not engage in relaxation procedures.   0 points

4. I get enough sleep daily to feel rested
    and energetic.   5 points

    I get enough sleep daily to feel somewhat
    rested and energetic.   3 points

I do not sleep enough to feel rested
or energetic.   0 points

5. I attend a formalized place of worship
   weekly.   5 points

   I attend a formalized place of worship
   monthly.   3 points

   I do not attend a formalized place of
   worship.   0 points

Spiritual Domain Total   _____/25

Diet and Nutrition

Circle the response that best describes your behavior during the past three months.

1. I eat several ounces of salmon two or
   more times a week.   5 points

   I eat salmon (or other fish listed in
   this text) one time a week.   3 points

   I do not eat fish.   0 points

2. I eat 2 cups of vegetables and fruits
   every day.   5 points

   I eat 2 cups of vegetables and fruits
   one time a week.   3 points

   I do not eat vegetables and fruits.   0 points

3. I drink one 4 to 6 ounce glass of red
   wine or grape juice daily.   5 points

   I drink one 4 to 6 ounce glass of red
   wine or grape juice weekly.   3 points

   I do not consume red wine or
   grape juice.   0 points

4. I eat two meals with utensils daily.   5 points

   I eat one meal with utensils daily.   3 points

   I do not use utensils on a daily basis.   0 points

5. I eat walnuts several times a week.   5 points

   I eat walnuts once or twice a month.   3 points

   I do not eat walnuts.   0 points

6. I consume 80% of the portions
    provided me as a rule.   5 points

    I consume 100% of the food on my plate.   3 points

    I tend to overeat regardless of portion size.   0 points

Total Diet and Nutrition Score   _____/30

Your Brain Health Scoreboard

Date	Physical	Mental	Social	Spiritual	Diet
Baseline Score	/ 25 = X 100 =	/35 = X 100 =	/25 = X 100 =	/ 25 = X 100 =	/30 = X 100 =
1st Quarter	/ 25 = X 100 =	/35 = X 100 =	/25 = X 100 =	/ 25 = X 100 =	/30 = X 100 =
2nd Quarter	/ 25 = X 100 =	/35 = X 100 =	/25 = X 100 =	/ 25 = X 100 =	/30 = X 100 =
3rd Quarter	/ 25 = X 100 =	/35 = X 100 =	/25 = X 100 =	/ 25 = X 100 =	/30 = X 100 =
4th Quarter	/25 = X 100 =	/35 = X 100 =	/25 = X 100 =	/ 25 = X 100 =	/30 = X 100 =
Annual Brain Health Score	/ 100 = X 100 =	/ 140 = X 100 =	/100 = X 100 =	/100 = X 100 =	/120 = X 100 =

HOW TO CALCULATE AND INTERPRET YOUR SCORES

1. To derive your *Quarterly Brain Health Score for each Domain*: Add the scores of your circled responses and insert the total score into the formula listed for each quarter.

2. To derive your *Quarterly Total Brain Health Score*: Add the total scores for each domain, divide by 140, and then multiply X 100.

3. To derive an *Annual Brain Health Score by Domain:* Add the four scores of each domain and apply that score to the formula listed for the Annual Brain Health Score for that particular domain.

   For example: Physical Health Domain:

   Total score for each quarter/100 X 100 = _____

4. To derive a *Grand Total for overall Brain Health for the year*: Add the five Annual Brain Health Scores together, divide by 560 and multiply by 100.

   Grand Total = (five Annual Brain Health Scores) / 560

   = _____

   X 100 = _____

INTERPRETATION OF YOUR SCORE

You may use the following guide to interpret each of your four scores described above:

100-90: Great job! Maintain your lifestyle approach.

89-80: Good Job! Make a few changes to improve your lifestyle.

79-70: Average Job. Consider making changes in several domains.

69-60: Poor Job. Significant change is needed in several domains.

59-50: Help! Re-assess the importance of your life story and attempt to make one small change in your lifestyle at a time.

APPENDIX 2

Daily Brain Health Activities

Physical Activity	Mental Stimulation	Spirituality	Socialization	Nutrition
Walk Daily	Board Games	Daily Prayer	Hobbies	Salmon
Aerobic Exercise	Read and Write	Meditate	Join a new Group	Herring and Mackerel
Dance	Sign Language	Relaxation Techniques	Dine with Others	Walnuts
Garden	Computer-based Products	Increase Sleep	Do not Retire	Colored Fruits
Knit	Travel	Learn to say "no"	Grow Network of Friends	Colored Vegetables
Use non-Dominant Side	Novel and Complex	Slow Down	Recreate and Laugh	Increase Antioxidants
Jog	Develop Language Skills	Yoga and Pilate	Be Forgiving	Eat 80% of Portion Served
Purchase a Pedometer	Learn a Musical Instrument	Attend Formal Place of Worship	Connect with Family	Use Utensils
Biking, Swimming, Light Weights	Listen to Classic Music	Identify Body Targets of Stress	Personal Mission in Life	Green Leafy Vegetables

*These are suggestions for activities to incorporate into your brain health lifestyle. As with any healthy lifestyle, disease can still occur.

APPENDIX THREE
3 Day Sample Menu Including Brain-Healthy Foods

Day 1	Day 2	Day 3

Breakfast:
1 cup oatmeal
  cooked with soy milk &
sprinkled
  with cinnamon
1 orange
4 oz unsweetened carrot
juice
 	
Snack:
1 plum
 	
Lunch:
3 oz grilled chicken breast
with topping
  ½ cup onion slices & ½
cup green
  bellpeppers, cooked
down in 1 tsp
  canola oil
1 small baked sweet
potato with skin
1 cup green beans
  cooked with 1 Tbsp
lemon juice &
  1 Tbsp almond slices
Unsweetened beverage
 	
Snack:
4 oz low-fat cottage
cheese
1 peach
 	
Dinner:
Southwestern Shrimp
Wrap
  3 oz grilled shrimp
  ½ cup black beans
cooked with 1
  Tbsp lime juice & ¼
tsp turmeric
  (add cayenne pepper if
desired)
  1 cup shredded
romaine lettuce
  1 whole grain flour
tortilla wrap
1 cup sliced tomatoes
1 cup skim milk
	Breakfast:
	Sunshine Smoothie
	  1 cup frozen (or fresh)
	mixed
	  berries, 4 oz
	unsweetened orange
	  juice, ½ banana, 6-oz
	container
	  light non-fat yogurt
	  and 2 tsp wheat
	  germ blended with
	ice.
	
	Snack:
	¼ cup pistachios
	
	Lunch:
	3 oz albacore tuna (fresh
	or canned)
	  Cooked as desired
	2 slices whole grain
	bread
	2 cups raw spinach salad
	topped with 2 Tbsp dried
	cranberries & 1 Tbsp
	olive oil vinaigrette
	  1 tsp olive oil
	  2 tsp vinegar
	  black pepper to taste
	Unsweetened beverage
	
	Snack:
	1 cup cubed cantaloupe
	1 6-oz container light
	non-fat yogurt
	
	Dinner:
	3 oz grilled beef sirloin
	2/3 cup steamed brown
	rice
	½ cup cooked collard
	greens
	½ cup cooked sliced
	beets
	1 cup skim milk
		Breakfast:
		1 cup toasted oats cereal
		6 oz soy milk
		4 oz unsweetened
		grapefruit juice
		
		Snack:
		2 kiwifruits
		
		Lunch:
		3 oz roasted turkey
		breast
		1 cup black-eyed peas
		½ cup steamed broccoli
		1 cup raw cabbage salad
		  shredded cabbage
		mixed with ½
		  cup raw shredded
		carrots and
		  1 Tbsp olive oil
		vinaigrette
		  (see recipe on Day 2)
		Unsweetened beverage
		
		Snack:
		2 Tbsp homemade
		hummus
		  cooked chickpeas
		mashed and
		  mixed with 1 fresh
		mashed garlic
		  clove & 1 tsp olive oil
		then
		  sprinkled with sesame
		seeds
		½ whole grain pita bread
		pocket
		
		Dinner:
		3 oz grilled salmon
		1 small potato with skin
		  mashed or baked
		6 asparagus stalks,
		broiled until tender
		1 cup skim milk

This menu represents a 3-day average of 1800 total calories per day and is intended as an example for the average-sized person.

Because everyone has unique medical nutritional needs like Diabetes or high blood pressure, please consult a Registered Dietitian for additional assistance with meal planning.

ABOUT THE AUTHORS

Lauren M. Dorgant

Lauren M. Dorgant is a Licensed and Registered Dietitian residing in Lake Charles, Louisiana. She obtained her Bachelor of Science degree in Dietetics from Louisiana State University and completed her Dietetic Internship at McNeese State University. Lauren is currently employed by a regional medical center in Lake Charles where she coordinates patient nutrition education though outpatient clinics, including Diabetes, CHF, hepatitis, oncology, as well as others. In addition, she teaches weight management classes along with diabetes and cardiac nutrition classes.

Lauren serves on the hospital's Diabetes Advisory Committee and is a member of the statewide Disease Management Initiative for Diabetes. A member of the American Association of Diabetes Educators and the American Dietetic Association, Lauren also currently serves as the president-elect of the Southwest chapter of the Louisiana Dietetic Association. In October of 2006, Lauren obtained her Certificate of Training in Adult Weight Management.

Being a Louisiana native, she realizes that food is an immeasurable component of our culture and that old habits are hard to break; specifically, the change of the traditional dietary habits of southern families. With novel emphasis on diet on the ever-important matter of brain health and functionality, Lauren works to promote healthier lifestyles through improved food choices.

Paul David Nussbaum, Ph.D.

Clinical Neuropsychologist
Adjunct Associate Professor of Neurological Surgery
University of Pittsburgh School of Medicine And
International Consultant on Aging and Brain Health

ageon@zoominternet.net
www.paulnussbaum.com
(412) 471-1195

Doctor Nussbaum is a licensed clinical neuropsychologist in the state of Pennsylvania. Having earned his Doctorate in clinical psychology from the University of Arizona in 1991, Dr. Nussbaum completed his internship and Post-Doctoral fellowship at Western Psychiatric Institute and Clinic, University of Pittsburgh School of Medicine. He is an adjunct Associate Professor in Neurological Surgery at the University of Pittsburgh School of Medicine.

Doctor Nussbaum has 20 years experience in the care of older persons suffering dementia and related disorders. From the outpatient setting to the long- term care setting, Dr. Nussbaum has worked in all sectors of the continuum of care. An expert in neuroanatomy and human behavior, Dr. Nussbaum has published many peer reviewed articles, books, and chapters within the scientific community. He is a national and international lecturer on brain health, healthy aging, dementia and related disorders.

Doctor Nussbaum educates the general public on the basics of the human brain and how to keep the brain healthy over the entire lifespan. He provides informative and fun keynote presentations across the nation and is often interviewed in the local and national press/media. Doctor Nussbaum also provides consultation to corporate America on brain health.

For more information about Brain health or to contact Dr. Nussbaum visit his website (*www.paulnussbaum.com*).

Maintain the Checkup for your Neck Up!!